Table of Contents

INTRODUCTION — 2

CHAPTER 1: INTRODUCTION TO THE DIGITAL ECONOMY — 5

CHAPTER 2: EVOLUTION AND HISTORY OF THE DIGITAL ECONOMY — 7

CHAPTER 3: KEY PLAYERS IN THE DIGITAL ECONOMY — 10

CHAPTER 4: DIGITAL BUSINESS MODELS AND PLATFORMS — 13

CHAPTER 5: E-COMMERCE AND DIGITAL MARKETPLACES — 16

CHAPTER 6: FINTECH AND DIGITAL FINANCE — 20

CHAPTER 7: DATA AND PRIVACY IN THE DIGITAL ECONOMY — 23

CHAPTER 8: ARTIFICIAL INTELLIGENCE AND AUTOMATION IN THE DIGITAL ECONOMY — 26

CHAPTER 9: BLOCKCHAIN AND DECENTRALIZED TECHNOLOGIES IN THE DIGITAL ECONOMY — 29

CHAPTER 10: THE GIG ECONOMY AND DIGITAL LABOR — 33

CHAPTER 11: DIGITAL MARKETING AND CUSTOMER ENGAGEMENT — 36

CHAPTER 12: THE ROLE OF INNOVATION AND DISRUPTION IN THE DIGITAL ECONOMY — 39

CHAPTER 13: GLOBALIZATION AND THE DIGITAL ECONOMY — 43

CHAPTER 14: CHALLENGES AND RISKS OF THE DIGITAL ECONOMY
46

CHAPTER 15: THE FUTURE OF THE DIGITAL ECONOMY **49**

CONCLUSION **52**

Digital Economy Q&A

by

Pinnacle Press

Introduction

Today's world is undeniably digital. From online shopping and remote work to social media and digital currencies, technology has transformed nearly every part of our lives, creating a new economic system: the digital economy. This system, powered by data, connectivity, and constant innovation, is reshaping industries, creating new jobs, and impacting global markets.

The digital economy includes all activities that rely on digital technology, from e-commerce and online financial services to AI and decentralized finance. It's more than just buying and selling online; it's a full ecosystem of digital infrastructure, data, platforms, and participants that add value to our lives.

This book will guide you through the key elements of the digital economy, exploring topics like e-commerce, fintech, artificial intelligence, blockchain, and the gig economy. We'll look at how these pieces form an interconnected system that's changing businesses, consumer habits, and governments. We'll also address the challenges that come with this transformation, such as cybersecurity, data privacy, regulations, and the digital divide.

The digital economy is not just about technology; it's a cultural and economic shift changing how we live, work, and interact. As digital tools keep evolving, staying informed and adaptable is crucial. This book aims to provide insights, practical advice, and a look at the future of the digital economy, helping you understand the forces shaping our digital world, the opportunities ahead, and our shared responsibility to ensure it remains a positive force. Welcome to the digital economy, where the future is already here, and the possibilities are endless.

Chapter 1: Introduction to the Digital Economy

1. What does "digital economy" mean?

Digital economy is about business activities using digital tools like the internet and smartphones. It's where goods, services, and information are created and shared through digital channels.

2. How has technology changed traditional business?

Technology lets businesses reach people worldwide through online platforms, instead of relying only on physical stores. This makes things faster and easier for both companies and customers.

3. Why is the Digital Economy Important?

The digital economy is a big part of our lives now. It makes businesses more efficient, creates new industries, and gives consumers more options and convenience.

4. What are the main parts of the digital economy?

Digital Infrastructure: Internet, mobile networks, and data centers.
Digital Platforms: Websites and apps where people buy and sell things.
Digital Payments: Ways to pay online, like digital wallets.
Data and Analytics: Information used to make business decisions.
Cybersecurity: Protects personal data and builds trust in online services.

5. How does the digital economy affect everyday life?

The digital economy is everywhere, from ordering food online to using apps for health tracking. It's made tasks easier and allows people to work, shop, and manage finances remotely.

6. Who benefits from the digital economy?

Consumers: More choices and better prices.
Businesses: New ways to reach people and work more efficiently.
Entrepreneurs: Easier entry into the market.
Workers: Remote work options and new job types.

7. What challenges come with the digital economy?

Data Privacy and Security: Protecting personal information.
Digital Divide: Not everyone has equal internet access.
Job Changes: Some jobs disappear while new ones require different skills.
Market Power: Big companies dominate certain areas.

8. How does the digital economy change different industries?

Retail: More online shopping, fewer physical stores.
Finance: Faster, easier digital payments and online banking.
Healthcare: Remote care and health tracking tools.
Education: Online learning offers flexible options.

9. Is the digital economy environmentally friendly?

The digital economy has pros and cons. Data centers use a lot of energy, but remote work can reduce travel, which is better for the environment.

10. What's the future of the digital economy?

The digital economy is always changing with new tech like AI and 5G. Staying informed and flexible will help people and businesses keep up.

Chapter 2: Evolution and History of the Digital Economy

1. When did the digital economy start?

The digital economy began in the second half of the 20th century, with early roots in the 1950s and 60s through computers and IT. It really took off in the 1990s when the internet became widely available.

2. What were the first digital businesses?

Early digital businesses focused on simple data processing and electronic transactions, like EFT in the 60s and 70s. By the 90s, e-commerce sites like Amazon and eBay began selling products online.

3. How did the internet change the digital economy?

The internet allowed instant global communication and access to information, making it possible for businesses to connect with people everywhere and offer services faster and more reliably.

4. What are some big milestones in the digital economy?

70s-80s: Digital transaction tools like EFT.
90s: World Wide Web and early e-commerce.
2000s: Broadband and mobile tech.
2007: iPhone launch, leading to mobile-first services.
2010s: Cloud computing and social media growth.
2020s: AI and blockchain development.

5. How did social media impact the digital economy?

Social media helped businesses connect with people more personally, enabling new marketing methods like influencer marketing. It also allowed small businesses to reach large audiences without big budgets.

6. How did mobile devices help the digital economy grow?

Smartphones, brought the internet to billions, enabling transactions, communication, and media on the go. This led to new services like Uber and other location-based apps.

7. What was the dot-com bubble, and how did it impact the digital economy?

The dot-com bubble saw a lot of investment in internet companies, many of which failed. However, it led to lasting digital infrastructure, and some companies, like Amazon, grew to dominate.

8. How has e-commerce changed over time?

E-commerce evolved from simple online shopping in the 90s to include mobile shopping, social commerce, and subscription services, which have transformed how people shop worldwide.

9. How did cloud computing change the digital economy?

Cloud computing made it easier and cheaper for businesses to access data storage and software, helping startups grow quickly and allowing businesses of all sizes to make data-driven decisions.

10. How did data analytics impact the digital economy?

Data analytics let companies understand customer preferences, improve services, and make better decisions, helping businesses across many industries stay competitive.

11. Why are digital payments important in the digital economy?

Digital payments made it easy and safe to pay online, which helped e-commerce grow. They continue to evolve with new options like digital wallets and cryptocurrencies.

12. How did the gig economy contribute to the digital economy?

The gig economy, powered by apps like Uber and Airbnb, created new work models, allowing flexible jobs and quick services that add convenience for consumers.

13. How has the digital economy spread globally?

The digital economy has become global, with even emerging markets joining. Mobile and affordable internet have helped connect these areas, creating new economic opportunities.

14. What are the latest trends in the digital economy?

The latest trends include AI, blockchain, IoT, and remote work, all of which are reshaping businesses and offering new ways to operate digitally.

Chapter 3: Key Players in the Digital Economy

1. Who are the major companies in the digital economy?

Major players include Apple, Amazon, Google, Meta (Facebook), and Microsoft. These companies shape how people use technology for shopping, social media, data, and cloud services.

2. How do big tech companies influence the market?

Tech giants have huge control over information and digital services. They set standards, manage access to large amounts of data, and often buy smaller companies to stay ahead.

3. What do startups contribute to the digital economy?

Startups drive new ideas and bring fresh business models, often shaking up traditional industries. Companies like Uber and Spotify started as small startups and changed entire markets.

4. How do investors support the digital economy?

Venture capitalists give startups the money and advice they need to grow. In return, they hope to profit if the startup succeeds, helping fuel growth in the digital economy.

5. How do governments and regulators Impact the digital economy?

Governments create rules to protect data privacy, security, and fair competition. They aim to balance growth with protecting consumers and fair competition.

6. How do consumers affect the digital economy?

Consumers drive demand by choosing which products and services succeed. Their data also helps companies understand trends, create better products, and personalize experiences.

7. What impact do digital platforms have on the economy?

Platforms like Amazon and Google connect people with products and information. They give businesses access to a big audience but also control what people see, impacting success.

8. How do cloud providers contribute to the digital economy?

Cloud providers like AWS and Microsoft Azure allow companies to store data and run apps online, making it easier and cheaper to scale up without physical servers.

9. What role do digital payment providers play?

Payment services like PayPal, Apple Pay, etc. make online payments quick and safe, enabling businesses to sell to people around the world.

10. How do content creators and influencers affect the digital economy?

Content creators connect directly with audiences, helping brands reach people in a personal way. Influencer marketing has become a major strategy for many businesses.

11. Why are gig workers important in the digital economy?

Gig workers provide flexible services on-demand, like rideshares and deliveries, meeting consumer needs quickly. This creates new work opportunities but also raises questions about job security.

12. How do data scientists and engineers impact the digital economy?

Data scientists and engineers **create** the technology behind digital services and analyze data to improve products and understand customers, helping companies work smarter and faster.

13. Why is cybersecurity important in the digital economy?

Cybersecurity experts protect businesses from cyber attacks and data breaches, building trust so consumers feel safe using digital services.

14. What are some challenges in the digital economy?

Challenges in the digital economy include tech giants facing privacy concerns, startups needing funding, governments creating balanced rules, and consumers dealing with privacy and choice overload.

Chapter 4: Digital Business Models and Platforms

1. What is a digital business model?

A digital business model is how a business creates and delivers value using digital tools, like online platforms and data networks. Examples include e-commerce, subscription services, and on-demand apps.

2. How are digital business models different from traditional ones?

Digital business models rely on technology to reach more people quickly and often need less physical space, which helps reduce costs. For example, e-commerce stores don't need physical shops.

3. What are the main digital business models?

E-commerce (selling online)
Subscription (monthly fees for access, like Netflix)
Freemium (free basic services with paid upgrades)
On-demand (instant services, like Uber)
Marketplace (connecting buyers and sellers, like eBay)
Advertising (free content funded by ads, like Facebook)

4. What are digital platforms, and why are they important?

Digital platforms are online spaces where people can connect, buy, and sell. Examples include Amazon for shopping, Facebook for social media, and Salesforce for business tools.

5. How do digital marketplaces operate?

Digital marketplaces connect buyers and sellers but don't usually hold stock. They earn money through transaction fees, subscriptions, or ads. Examples include Amazon, Etsy, and Alibaba.

6. What Are the benefits of subscription models?

Subscriptions offer steady income, helping businesses plan and improve services over time. Examples are Netflix for streaming and Dollar Shave Club for monthly products.

7. How does the freemium model work?

The freemium model offers a free basic service and charges for extra features.

8. What are the advantages of on-demand platforms?

On-demand platforms provide services instantly, offering convenience.

9. How do advertising-based models make money?

Advertising-based models offer free content or services and charge advertisers to show ads to users. Facebook and Google make most of their money this way.

10. What are aggregator (models)?

Aggregators collect options from different sources to present them in one place, like Kayak for travel bookings or Yelp for local business reviews.

11. What are some challenges for digital businesses?

Some challenges include heavy competition, customer retention, data privacy concerns, and scaling costs as businesses grow.

12. How do digital platforms monetize data?

Digital platforms analyze user data to improve products, personalize ads, and sometimes sell insights to other companies, like social media platforms that use data for targeted ads.

13. What is a hybrid digital business model?

A hybrid digital business model combines different approaches. For example, Amazon mixes e-commerce and a marketplace, while LinkedIn combines freemium, subscription, and advertising.

14. How do digital ecosystems create value?

Ecosystems like Apple's connect various products and services, creating a seamless experience that encourages loyalty and makes the system more valuable for users.

15. What are network effects?

Network effects occur when a platform becomes more valuable as more people use it. For instance, more users on Facebook lead to more content and engagement.

16. What are examples of successful digital business models?

Successful digital business models include Amazon (e-commerce), Netflix (subscription), LinkedIn (freemium), eBay (marketplace), and Uber (on-demand).

17. How do digital businesses adapt to consumer changing needs?

Digital businesses use data and feedback to update their offerings and personalize experiences, like Netflix adjusting recommendations based on viewing history.

18. What are future trends for digital business models?

Likely trends include more personalized services, expanded use of blockchain, bundled subscriptions, virtual reality experiences, and eco-friendly business practices.

Chapter 5: E-commerce and Digital Marketplaces

1. What is e-commerce?

E-commerce is buying and selling goods or services online. It allows businesses to reach people globally with minimal physical setup.

2. What are the main types of e-commerce?

B2C (Business-to-Consumer): Businesses selling to individual consumers (like Amazon).
B2B (Business-to-Business): Businesses selling to other businesses (like Alibaba).
C2C (Consumer-to-Consumer): Individuals selling to each other (like eBay).
C2B (Consumer-to-Business): Consumers offering services to businesses (like Upwork).

3. How do digital marketplaces work?

Digital marketplaces connect buyers and sellers but don't usually hold stock. They make money through fees or commissions. Examples are Amazon and Etsy.

4. What are the advantages of e-commerce for consumers?

E-commerce offers convenience, a wide range of products, easy price comparisons, and personalized recommendations.

5. How does e-commerce help businesses?

E-commerce lowers costs, expands reach to global customers, provides data insights, and allows quick scaling.

6. What are different e-commerce business models?

Direct-to-Consumer (DTC): Selling directly to customers.
Drop Shipping: Selling products that are fulfilled by a third party.
Wholesale: Selling in bulk to other businesses.
White Labeling: Branding generic products as unique to the business.

7. How has mobile commerce (M-commerce) changed e-commerce?

M-commerce is shopping on smartphones and tablets, making it easy to shop on the go. Apps like Amazon have optimized for mobile use.

8. What is social commerce?

Social commerce is shopping through social media platforms. Platforms like Instagram allow in-app purchases, combining social interaction with e-commerce.

9. How do payment gateways and digital wallets work?

Payment gateways like Stripe and digital wallets like Apple Pay process secure payments, making checkout easier and faster.

10. How are logistics and fulfillment managed by e-commerce businesses?

E-commerce businesses can manage logistics themselves, use third-party services, or rely on networks like Amazon FBA for storage and delivery.

11. What challenges does e-commerce face?

Challenges include high shipping costs, managing returns, data privacy, and cybersecurity to prevent fraud.

12. How do e-commerce platforms use data?

E-commerce platforms analyze data to make personalized recommendations, improve products, and optimize marketing strategies.

13. What are popular tools for e-commerce?

Platforms like Shopify, WooCommerce, BigCommerce, and Magento help businesses create and manage online stores.

14. What's the difference between Amazon and a personal website?

Marketplaces offer a bigger audience but more competition, while personal sites give businesses full control over branding and customer experience.

15. What is omnichannel retailing?

Omnichannel retailing is selling across multiple channels like websites, apps, and stores to create a seamless shopping experience.

16. How do e-commerce businesses manage customer relationships?

E-commerce businesses use CRM tools to track interactions and preferences, helping personalize communication and build loyalty.

17. What are legal and ethical issues in e-commerce?

Legal and ethical issues include data privacy, transparent pricing, and fair return policies.

18. What are the environmental impacts of e-commerce?

E-commerce can reduce the need for physical stores but can increase packaging waste and transport emissions. Some businesses use eco-friendly practices to lessen these impacts.

19. How is AI used in e-commerce?

AI helps personalize shopping experiences, predict customer needs, and automate tasks, like chatbots for customer service.

20. What does the future look like for e-commerce?

Trends include voice shopping, augmented reality for product previews, sustainable practices, and faster delivery with drones and autonomous vehicles.

Chapter 6: Fintech and Digital Finance

1. What is fintech?

Fintech, or financial technology, uses digital tools to improve financial services, like payments, lending, and investing. It has made finance faster, more accessible, and more innovative.

2. How does fintech differ from traditional banking?

Fintech provides faster, more affordable services and often offers online-only options, reducing the need for physical branches and focusing on user experience.

3. What types of services does fintech offer?

Digital Payments (e.g., PayPal)
Digital Lending
Robo-Advisors (e.g., Betterment)
Blockchain and Cryptocurrencies (e.g., Bitcoin),
Insurtech (e.g., Lemonade for insurance).

4. How do digital payment systems work?

Payment systems like Stripe handle secure online transactions, while digital wallets, like Apple Pay, store payment details for easy purchases.

5. How does blockchain work in fintech?

Blockchain securely records transactions without intermediaries, allowing for cryptocurrencies, smart contracts, and decentralized finance (DeFi).

6. What are cryptocurrencies?

Cryptocurrencies, like Bitcoin, are digital currencies using blockchain to enable secure, peer-to-peer transactions without a central authority.

7. What Is Decentralized Finance (DeFi)?

DeFi uses blockchain to recreate financial services (like lending) without banks, offering transparency and lower costs but facing security challenges.

8. How do robo-advisors work?

Robo-advisors use algorithms to manage investments based on user goals, offering affordable, automated advice for investors.

9. How has Fintech improved financial inclusion?

Fintech provides access to banking, lending, and payment tools for those without traditional bank accounts, promoting financial inclusion.

10. How does Buy Now, Pay Later (BNPL) work?

BNPL lets consumers buy items and pay later in installments, often interest-free if paid on time. Examples include Klarna and Afterpay.

11. What are Central Bank Digital Currencies (CBDCs)?

CBDCs are digital forms of national currencies issued by central banks, offering secure, government-backed digital payments.

12. How do fintech companies use data and AI?

Fintech companies use data and AI to personalize services, detect fraud, and assess credit. For example, AI can spot unusual spending that might indicate fraud.

13. What are the security risks in fintech?

Risks include data breaches and fraud. Fintechs use encryption and authentication to protect users, following data privacy regulations.

14. What is regtech?

Regtech uses technology to help fintech companies follow financial regulations efficiently, automating tasks like risk assessment.

15. What is Peer-to-Peer (P2P) lending?

P2P lending connects borrowers directly with lenders online, often offering better rates than traditional loans. Examples include LendingClub.

16. How do mobile banking apps work?

Mobile apps let users manage their accounts, transfer funds, and pay bills on their smartphones, increasing accessibility and convenience.

17. How are digital wallets used?

Digital wallets store payment info, allowing contactless payments via smartphone. Examples include Apple Pay and Google Pay.

18. What are the risks and challenges in Fintech?

The risks and challenges are regulatory compliance, cybersecurity, consumer trust, and ensuring financial stability amid rapid growth.

19. How are banks adapting to fintech?

Banks are creating digital services, partnering with fintechs, and using mobile apps to compete and stay relevant.

20. What trends may shape fintech's future?

Future trends include more DeFi, increased AI and automation, embedded finance in apps, sustainable finance products, and fintech expansion in emerging markets.

Chapter 7: Data and Privacy in the Digital Economy

1. Why is data so valuable in the digital economy?

Data is essential for insights, decision-making, and innovation. It allows companies to understand customers, improve services, and gain competitive advantages.

2. How do companies gather data?

Companies gather data through website interactions, social media, surveys, connected devices, and sometimes by buying data from other sources.

3. What do companies use data for?

Data helps with personalization, targeted marketing, predicting trends, optimizing operations, and developing products to better meet customer needs.

4. What are some privacy issues with data use?

Key concerns include data tracking, misuse, sharing with third parties, and data breaches, all of which raise questions about transparency and user consent.

5. What does data privacy mean?

Data privacy involves protecting personal information from misuse and giving people control over how their data is collected, used, and shared.

6. What are the effects of data breaches?

Data breaches can lead to financial losses, loss of consumer trust, identity theft, and regulatory penalties, impacting both companies and individuals.

7. Why is consent important for data privacy?

Consent ensures users are aware of how their data will be used and agree to it, building trust and allowing control over personal information.

8. How does data enable personalization?

Companies use data to tailor products, ads, and content to individual preferences, like recommending products or curating playlists.

9. How do anonymization and encryption work?

Anonymization removes personal details from data, while encryption makes data unreadable without special access, protecting individual privacy.

10. What are cookies in digital privacy?

Cookies track user behavior on websites. They improve user experience but can raise privacy concerns if used without clear consent.

11. How does AI use data, and what are the privacy implications?

AI relies on data to make predictions and recommendations but can also reveal unintended insights about individuals, raising privacy risks.

12. What are data ethics?

Data ethics involve using data responsibly and transparently, with fairness and respect for users' privacy and rights.

13. What are the challenges of following privacy laws?

Compliance is costly and complex, especially for global companies that must meet different standards in various regions.

14. How can consumers protect their data privacy?

Consumers can use strong passwords, two-factor authentication, limit data sharing, and use privacy-focused tools like VPNs.

15. What measures do companies take to secure data?

Companies use firewalls, encryption, access controls, and regular audits to keep data safe from unauthorized access.

16. What is data governance?

Data governance is the framework for managing data accurately and securely, helping businesses comply with regulations and use data responsibly.

17. How Do New Technologies Affect Data Privacy?

New technologies collect vast data, raising new privacy challenges and requiring advanced protections to keep data secure.

18. What happens when a user requests data deletion?

Many laws allow users to request data removal. Companies must delete the data and confirm compliance within a set timeframe.

19. What Is the Future of Data Privacy?

The future may bring privacy-first tools, more control for users, AI regulations, reliance on voluntarily shared data, and greater transparency in data practices.

Chapter 8: Artificial Intelligence and Automation in the Digital Economy

1. What Is Artificial Intelligence (AI) in the Digital Economy?

AI allows machines to perform tasks that usually need human intelligence, like learning and decision-making. In the digital economy, AI powers tools like recommendation engines and chatbots, enhancing efficiency and personalization.

2. What's the difference between automation and AI?

Automation handles tasks without human input, often repeating actions, while AI-based automation can learn and adapt. Basic automation handles routine tasks, whereas AI can analyze data and make decisions.

3. How is AI used in digital business?

AI is used for personalized recommendations, chatbots, image and speech recognition, fraud detection, and predictive analytics to improve customer experience and security.

4. What Is Machine Learning (ML) in AI?

ML enables systems to learn from data without specific programming, allowing them to improve over time. It helps with personalization, fraud detection, and optimizing decisions.

5. How does AI make personalization better?

AI analyzes user data to customize products, ads, and content for individual preferences, leading to more engaging experiences.

6. How does AI improve customer service?

AI powers chatbots and virtual assistants that respond quickly to customer inquiries, allowing human agents to focus on more complex issues.

7. How does AI help with data analysis?

AI analyzes large datasets to reveal patterns and insights, helping businesses make informed decisions and predict trends.

8. What are autonomous systems?

Autonomous systems, like self-driving cars and delivery drones, operate independently using AI and sensors to make real-time decisions.

9. What is RPA, and how does it help?

RPA automates repetitive tasks like data entry, saving time and reducing errors in fields like finance and healthcare.

10. How is AI used to detect fraud?

AI detects unusual patterns in transactions that may indicate fraud, protecting consumers and businesses in banking and online services.

11. What is predictive maintenance?

AI monitors equipment to predict maintenance needs, reducing downtime and repair costs, especially in industries like manufacturing.

12. How does AI help with hiring?

AI screens resumes and assesses candidate fit, speeding up recruitment while reducing bias in the process.

13. What are the ethical concerns with AI?

Ethical concerns include bias, lack of transparency, privacy risks, and job displacement, requiring responsible AI practices to ensure fairness.

14. Is AI regulated?

AI regulation is evolving and new AI-specific regulations are being considered and developed.

15. What impact does AI have on jobs?

AI can automate repetitive tasks, leading to job changes, but also creates demand for roles in AI, data science, and ethics.

16. How does AI enhance cybersecurity?

AI detects and responds to unusual activity, helping prevent cyberattacks and keeping data secure.

17. What Is Natural Language Processing (NLP)?

NLP helps machines understand human language, powering chatbots, voice assistants, and translation tools.

18. Why are AI ethics frameworks important?

AI ethics frameworks guide responsible AI use, promoting fairness, accountability, and privacy in AI development.

19. What are some risks of using AI?

Some risks of using AI include data dependency, complexity, and potential security vulnerabilities, which require careful management and testing.

20. What is the future of AI and automation?

The future includes AI-augmented work, explainable AI, edge AI, and increased use of AI in healthcare, education, and environmental solutions.

Chapter 9: Blockchain and Decentralized Technologies in the Digital Economy

1. What is blockchain?

Blockchain is a decentralized ledger that records transactions securely and transparently across a network of computers. Once data is added, it cannot be altered, creating a trusted, tamper-proof record.

2. How does blockchain work?

Blockchain uses a peer-to-peer network where transactions are verified by multiple participants (nodes) before being added. This consensus ensures accuracy and security, with cryptography protecting data from tampering.

3. What are the key features of blockchain?

Key features of blockchain include decentralization, immutability, transparency, and security, making blockchain ideal for applications requiring trust, security, and transparency.

4. What are cryptocurrencies?

Cryptocurrencies are digital assets like Bitcoin, using blockchain for secure, decentralized transactions. They serve as alternatives to traditional currency.

5. How is Ethereum different from Bitcoin?

Ethereum allows developers to create applications and smart contracts on its blockchain, while Bitcoin is primarily a digital currency.

6. What are smart contracts?

Smart contracts are self-executing contracts with terms coded on a blockchain. They automatically execute actions when specific conditions are met, reducing the need for intermediaries.

7. What is Decentralized Finance (DeFi)?

DeFi recreates financial services (like lending and trading) on blockchain, allowing transactions without banks or intermediaries, making financial services more accessible.

8. How do Decentralized Exchanges (DEXs) work?

DEXs enable peer-to-peer cryptocurrency trading without a central authority. Smart contracts handle transactions, providing privacy and security.

9. What are Non-Fungible Tokens (NFTs)?

NFTs are unique digital assets representing ownership of items like art or music. Each NFT is distinct, making it valuable for verifying digital ownership.

10. How Is Blockchain used in supply chain management?

Blockchain records each step of the supply process, enhancing transparency and traceability, reducing fraud, and improving accountability.

11. How does blockchain enhance privacy and security?

Blockchain decentralizes and encrypts data, making it difficult to alter or hack, giving users more control over their information.

12. What is tokenization?

Tokenization represents physical or digital assets as digital tokens on a blockchain, allowing for easier, fractional ownership and trading of assets.

13. What are blockchain consensus mechanisms?

Blockchain consensus mechanisms are methods like Proof of Work (PoW) and Proof of Stake (PoS) that validate transactions, ensuring network security and data integrity.

14. Why is blockchain criticized for environmental impact?

Some blockchains, like Bitcoin's, use energy-intensive methods (PoW) for validation. Alternatives like PoS are more eco-friendly.

15. What Is a Decentralized Autonomous Organization (DAO)?

A DAO is an organization governed by smart contracts and community voting rather than traditional management, allowing decentralized decision-making.

16. How does blockchain help with identity verification?

Blockchain securely stores digital identities, reducing fraud by giving users control over their personal information.

17. What challenges does blockchain face?

Challenges include scalability, regulatory uncertainty, interoperability between blockchains, and user-friendliness.

18. How are governments reacting to blockchain?

Reactions vary, with some exploring digital currencies and identity solutions, while others focus on regulations for crypto and DeFi.

19. What are Layer 2 solutions?

Layer 2 solutions are protocols built on existing blockchains to improve scalability and reduce fees, making blockchains faster and more affordable.

20. What might the future hold for blockchain?

Cross-chain interoperability, more DeFi adoption, expanded tokenized assets, privacy-focused solutions, and sustainable blockchain practices.

Chapter 10: The Gig Economy and Digital Labor

1. What Is the Gig Economy?

The gig economy is a labor market of short-term and freelance work, where individuals take on flexible roles through platforms like Uber, Upwork, and TaskRabbit.

2. How is gig work different from regular jobs?

Gig workers are usually independent contractors, lacking benefits like health insurance and paid leave, unlike traditional full-time employees.

3. What kinds of jobs are in the gig economy?

Ride-sharing (Uber), freelancing (Upwork), manual labor (TaskRabbit), and online gigs (Amazon Mechanical Turk).

4. How do platforms support the gig economy?

Platforms connect gig workers with clients, manage payments, and facilitate work matching, allowing gig work to scale rapidly.

5. How has technology helped the gig economy grow?

Mobile apps, digital payments, and cloud computing make it easy for people to find and complete work from anywhere.

6. What benefits does gig work offer individuals?

Gig work offers flexibility, diverse job options, autonomy, and a way to earn extra income.

7. What Are the downsides of gig work for Individuals?

The downsides of gig work for individuals include lack of benefits, income instability, limited job protections, and potential isolation.

8. How does gig work help businesses?

Gig work allows businesses to save on costs, scale easily, access diverse talent, and hire for specific projects without long-term commitments.

9. What challenges do businesses face in managing gig workers?

Issues include quality control, building loyalty, navigating legal compliance, and training gig workers.

10. Why are ratings important for gig workers?

Ratings impact a worker's reputation and job opportunities, as high ratings can lead to more work, while low ratings can limit access.

11. What legal issues do gig workers face?

Worker classification is debated, as it affects access to benefits, job protections, and tax obligations, with laws varying by region.

12. How do gig workers handle taxes?

Gig workers must track income and expenses and manage their own tax filings, often receiving tax documents from platforms.

13. How has the gig economy changed employment?

The gig economy has shifted work toward flexible, project-based arrangements, allowing people to manage multiple income sources.

14. How has the gig economy affected traditional sectors?

The gig economy disrupts industries like transportation and hospitality, prompting traditional businesses to adopt flexible work models.

15. How does the gig economy influence work-life balance?

The gig economy allows flexible scheduling, but income instability can pressure workers to put in more hours to meet earnings needs.

16. How does automation impact gig work?

Automation streamlines tasks like delivery but can also replace certain jobs, while creating new opportunities in tech and AI fields.

17. How do gig workers handle lack of benefits?

Many gig workers supplement income from multiple sources, buy private insurance, or seek alternate income to achieve financial security.

18. Are there unions for gig workers?

Yes, unions and advocacy groups are forming to improve pay, benefits, and protections, influencing policy and platform practices.

19. What does the future hold for the gig economy?

The future may bring more worker protections, portable benefits, automation in low-skill jobs, more professional gigs, and hybrid employment models, balancing flexibility with fair worker rights.

Chapter 11: Digital Marketing and Customer Engagement

1. What is digital marketing?

Digital marketing promotes products or services through online channels like search engines, social media, email, and websites, allowing real-time engagement and personalization to build customer relationships.

2. What are the main parts of digital marketing?

SEO (improving search engine rankings),
Content Marketing (creating valuable content),
Social Media Marketing (engaging on platforms like Instagram),
Email Marketing (targeted messaging), and
Paid Advertising (running ads on search and social platforms).

3. What is SEO, and how does it help?

SEO optimizes a website to rank higher in search results, using keywords, quality content, and backlinks to attract organic traffic and increase visibility.

4. Why is content marketing important?

Content marketing attracts and engages customers with valuable information, building trust and establishing the brand as an authority.

5. How do businesses use social media marketing?

Social media allows brands to connect with customers, promote products, and build community through platforms like Facebook, Instagram, and LinkedIn.

6. How does influencer marketing work?

Brands partner with influencers who recommend products to their followers, reaching new audiences and building credibility.

7. What role does email play in customer engagement?

Email marketing helps retain customers by sending personalized offers, product updates, and recommendations to subscribers.

8. How does data analytics improve marketing?

Analytics track customer behavior and campaign performance, helping marketers refine strategies for better results.

9. What are PPC campaigns?

PPC (pay-per-click) ads appear on search engines and social media, where businesses pay only when users click, attracting immediate traffic.

10. How does retargeting work?

Retargeting shows ads to people who visited a site but didn't convert, reminding them of the brand and encouraging them to return.

11. Why is personalization important?

Personalization tailors content and offers based on user preferences, making customers feel valued and improving engagement.

12. What is marketing automation?

Marketing automation software handles repetitive tasks like sending emails, saving time and ensuring messages reach the right audience.

13. How does CRM support marketing?

CRM systems store data on customer interactions, helping businesses personalize communications and improve retention.

14. What is affiliate marketing?

Affiliate marketing pays affiliates a commission for promoting a brand's products, expanding reach with minimal upfront cost.

15. Why is video marketing effective?

Video content is memorable and engaging, making it ideal for demonstrating products and telling brand stories.

16. How does voice search optimization work?

Voice search optimization tailors content for voice-activated devices, using natural language to meet users' spoken queries.

17. What do chatbots do?

Chatbots provide instant responses to questions on websites or apps, improving customer experience and offering 24/7 support.

18. Why is data privacy important?

Data privacy laws protect user rights, requiring transparency about data collection to build trust and comply with regulations.

19. What metrics measure digital marketing?

Metrics include conversion rate, click-through rate, ROI, customer acquisition cost, and engagement rate, indicating campaign effectiveness.

20. What trends are shaping digital marketing's future?

Future trends include greater personalization, augmented reality, voice and visual search, sustainability marketing, and privacy-focused strategies, making marketing more interactive and customer-centered.

Chapter 12: The Role of Innovation and Disruption in the Digital Economy

1. What Is Innovation in the Digital Economy?

Innovation is the creation of new technologies, ideas, or methods to improve products, services, or processes. It can be gradual (incremental) or groundbreaking (radical), helping businesses grow and adapt.

2. What are the main types of innovation?

Incremental Innovation: Small, continuous improvements (e.g., software updates).
Disruptive Innovation: Innovations that create new markets (e.g., streaming services).
Radical Innovation: Groundbreaking changes introducing entirely new solutions (e.g., blockchain).
Architectural Innovation: Combining existing technologies in new ways (e.g., AI in healthcare).

3. What is disruption and how does it affect industries?

Disruption occurs when new technologies or models challenge traditional ways, often forcing established businesses to adapt or risk losing relevance.

4. What are some examples of disruption in the digital economy?

Examples include streaming services like Netflix, e-commerce giants like Amazon, ride-sharing services like Uber, and fintech platforms like PayPal.

5. How do companies use innovation to stay competitive?

Companies invest in new technologies, improve customer experiences, and adopt new business models to stay relevant and competitive in fast-changing markets.

6. What is open innovation?

Open innovation involves collaborating with external sources, like customers or startups, to bring in new ideas and speed up innovation.

7. What role does digital transformation play in innovation?

Digital transformation integrates digital tools across business operations, enhancing productivity and creating new innovation opportunities.

8. Role of Research and Development (R&D) in Innovation

R&D allows companies to experiment and create new solutions, keeping them ahead of trends and improving competitiveness.

9. What role does venture capital play in innovation?

Venture capital funds startups with high growth potential, enabling them to scale and bring disruptive ideas to market.

10. What Is Customer-Centric Innovation?

Customer-centric innovation tailors products to meet specific customer needs, enhancing satisfaction and loyalty.

11. What is design thinking?

Design thinking is a method that focuses on understanding user needs, brainstorming, prototyping, and refining ideas to create practical, user-centered solutions.

12. How do companies encourage innovation?

Companies create innovative cultures by supporting creativity, risk-taking, and collaboration, allowing employees to try new ideas.

13. What are the risks of pursuing innovation?

Risks include high R&D costs, market uncertainty, regulatory challenges, and competition from established players.

14. How does Artificial Intelligence (AI) support innovation?

AI helps with data analysis, automation, and insights, accelerating product development and enabling personalized customer experiences.

15. How do startups disrupt established industries?

Startups often offer more efficient or affordable solutions, forcing traditional companies to innovate or risk becoming obsolete.

16. How does globalization affect innovation?

Globalization allows access to diverse talent and ideas, encouraging cross-border innovation and expanding markets.

17. How do established companies respond to disruption?

Established companies may acquire startups, create innovation labs, form partnerships, or modernize technology to stay competitive.

18. Why is sustainable innovation important?

Sustainable innovation focuses on eco-friendly practices, appealing to environmentally conscious consumers and meeting regulatory requirements.

19. How do blockchain and 5G enable innovation?

Blockchain provides secure transactions, and 5G offers faster connectivity, supporting new innovations like IoT and autonomous vehicles.

20. What trends will shape future innovation?

Trends include AI-driven solutions, decentralized models, sustainable practices, human-centered design, and more collaboration, all driving growth and transformation in the digital economy.

Chapter 13: Globalization and the Digital Economy

1. How has globalization influenced the digital economy?

Globalization allows businesses to reach international markets, access global talent, and operate across borders with the help of digital technologies like e-commerce and cloud computing.

2. How do digital platforms support globalization?

Platforms like Amazon, Alibaba, and Facebook connect people globally, enabling communication, transactions, and partnerships across borders.

3. How does e-commerce support international trade?

E-commerce lets businesses reach global audiences without physical stores, allowing even small companies to sell internationally through online marketplaces.

4. What are the benefits of globalization for businesses?

Benefits include access to new markets, cost reduction through outsourcing, a larger talent pool, and economies of scale.

5. How does globalization affect consumer choices?

Globalization gives consumers access to a wider range of products from around the world, making them expect variety, convenience, and quick access to global goods.

6. How do businesses adapt to different cultures and regulations?

Businesses localize products, adjust marketing strategies, and comply with regional laws on issues like data privacy and taxation.

7. How do cross-border payments support globalization?

Systems like PayPal and Stripe facilitate international transactions by converting currencies and providing secure payment options.

8. How does digital marketing adapt to global audiences?

Digital marketing uses geo-targeting, localization, and region-specific platforms to make content relevant and engaging for different cultures.

9. How does globalization impact jobs?

Globalization creates opportunities in fields like tech and customer service but can lead to job displacement in industries affected by outsourcing.

10. How does globalization promote innovation?

Globalization enables collaboration across countries, combining diverse perspectives to create innovative solutions and share expertise globally.

11. What are the environmental effects of a globalized digital economy?

The globalized digital economy reduces the need for physical goods but increases packaging waste and transportation emissions from e-commerce.

12. What is the digital divide, and why does it matter?

The digital divide is the gap between those with and without access to digital technology, limiting economic opportunities in underserved areas.

13. How do trade policies affect digital businesses?

Policies like tariffs and data privacy laws can complicate global operations, requiring companies to comply with different regulations.

14. Why is Intellectual Property (IP) protection important in globalization?

IP laws protect innovations across borders, helping businesses operate globally without risking unauthorized use of their technology.

15. What are the challenges of global operations?

Challenges include currency fluctuations, political instability, cybersecurity risks, and cultural misalignment.

16. How does globalization impact education?

Globalization expands access to online courses and training, helping people worldwide acquire skills valued in the global economy.

17. How do emerging markets contribute to the digital economy?

Regions like Asia and Africa are rapidly adopting digital technologies, creating new growth opportunities for global businesses.

18. How does remote work support globalization?

Remote work enables companies to hire talent globally, providing employees flexibility to work for international firms from anywhere.

19. Why is localization important?

Localization adapts products and marketing to fit cultural and linguistic needs, helping businesses relate with local audiences.

20. What are future trends for globalization?

Future trends include more inclusive globalization, sustainable practices, standardized regulations, cross-border innovation, and growth in emerging markets, shaping an interconnected digital economy.

Chapter 14: Challenges and Risks of the Digital Economy

1. What are the biggest challenges in the digital economy?

The biggest challenges include cybersecurity threats, privacy concerns, regulatory issues, and economic inequality, all of which impact businesses, governments, and consumers.

2. Why is cybersecurity important in the digital economy?

Cybersecurity protects data, finances, and reputations, ensuring business continuity by defending against threats like data breaches, phishing, and ransomware.

3. What are common cybersecurity threats?

Common cybersecurity threats include phishing, malware, ransomware, and DDoS attacks, each of which can damage systems, steal data, or disrupt services.

4. Why is data privacy important?

Consumers are concerned about how their data is used and stored, so respecting privacy helps build trust and avoid legal issues.

5. What are the regulatory issues for digital businesses?

Regulatory issues include compliance with data protection laws, digital taxes, and labor laws, which vary across countries and impact global operations.

6. Does the digital economy create inequality?

Yes, those without access to digital technology or skills miss out on job opportunities, widening the digital divide and economic inequality.

7. Why is the digital divide a problem?

Digital divide is a problem because the gap between those with and without access to digital technology limits opportunities in jobs, education, and services for under-resourced communities.

8. What are the ethical concerns in the digital economy?

Ethical concerns include data privacy, AI bias, misinformation, and fair treatment of gig workers, all of which impact trust and social responsibility.

9. How does automation affect jobs?

Automation replaces certain jobs, leading to displacement in fields like retail and customer service, making reskilling essential for future work.

10. How does the digital economy impact the environment?

While digital services reduce some resource needs, data centers, e-commerce logistics, and electronic waste contribute to pollution and resource strain.

11. Why is reliance on platforms risky?

Reliance on platforms like Amazon and Google can limit control, reduce margins, and increase vulnerability to platform policies and fees.

12. What are the risks of big tech monopolies?

Big tech monopolies can limit competition, stifle innovation, and lead to higher prices, impacting both businesses and consumers.

13. What are the effects of digital fraud?

Digital fraud harms businesses with financial losses and reputational damage, while consumers face financial hardship and potential identity theft.

14. Why is Intellectual Property (IP) protection important?

IP issues like software piracy and copyright infringement risk lost revenue and competitive disadvantages for creators and innovators.

15. How does rapid tech change affect businesses?

Companies must adapt quickly or risk becoming obsolete, though rapid adoption can sometimes lead to security vulnerabilities.

16. How do businesses handle online customer relationships?

Digital customer relationships require fast, seamless support to meet high expectations and avoid potential reputational damage from negative reviews.

17. How can businesses manage online reputational risks?

Proactive reputation management, transparent communication, and responsive customer service help protect a brand's image.

18. What are the risks of data dependency?

Data dependency can lead to privacy violations, regulatory scrutiny, and security risks, making effective data governance essential.

19. What are the legal challenges of global business?

Global business require compliance with diverse laws, including tax regulations, data privacy, and import/export rules.

20. How can businesses manage digital risks?

Business can manage digital risks by effective strategies include investing in cybersecurity, implementing data governance, staying compliant with regulations, diversifying revenue, reskilling employees, and adopting sustainable practices. These steps help build resilience and protect business assets and reputation.

Chapter 15: The Future of the Digital Economy

1. What trends are expected to shape the digital economy's future?

Key trends include increased automation, growth in decentralized finance (DeFi), a focus on sustainability, remote work, and personalized, customer-centric models.

2. How will AI impact the future digital economy?

AI will drive innovation in automation, customer service, predictive analytics, and personalization, particularly in healthcare, finance, and retail.

3. How will blockchain affect the future digital economy?

Blockchain is expected to expand beyond cryptocurrency, impacting areas like supply chains, voting, digital identity, and finance by increasing transparency and reducing intermediaries.

4. What impact will quantum computing have on the digital economy?

Quantum computing will revolutionize fields like cryptography and AI by solving complex problems faster than traditional computers, though widespread use may still be years away.

5. How will 5G influence the digital economy?

5G's fast, low-latency connections will support IoT, autonomous vehicles, and real-time data processing, creating new opportunities across industries.

6. How will sustainability shape the digital economy?

Businesses will focus on eco-friendly practices, such as energy-efficient data centers and sustainable supply chains, responding to consumer demand for transparency in sustainability.

7. What will the future of work look like?

Remote work, digital skills, and flexible hybrid models will become more common, and automation will require workers to reskill for new digital roles.

8. How will the digital economy address inequality?

Expanding internet access, improving digital literacy, and inclusive policies will help bridge the digital divide and create equitable opportunities.

9. What role will ethics play in AI's future?

Responsible AI practices focused on fairness, transparency, and privacy will help prevent bias and misuse, building trust among users.

10. How will the gig economy change?

The gig economy will grow, with more freelancers working globally, and policy changes may offer gig workers more rights and benefits.

11. What's the future of data privacy?

Stricter regulations on data privacy, combined with privacy-enhancing technologies, will protect user data and uphold consumer trust.

12. How will AR and VR shape industries?

AR and VR will create immersive experiences in gaming, education, and retail, allowing users to interact with products and environments virtually.

13. How will digital currencies evolve?

Digital currencies will gain traction, improving cross-border payments and adding secure, digital payment options.

14. What are super apps, and how will they impact users?

Super apps like WeChat integrate services like messaging, shopping, and payments in one platform, streamlining user experiences.

15. How will businesses approach innovation?

Businesses will use agile models, focus on sustainability, and prioritize ethical practices to stay competitive in the evolving digital economy.

16. What skills will be essential in the digital economy?

Skills in technology, data analysis, cybersecurity, creativity, and adaptability will be crucial, along with lifelong learning.

17. How will IoT influence the digital economy?

IoT will optimize operations, enhance user experiences, and drive innovation in smart homes, healthcare, and urban planning.

18. How will global collaboration evolve?

Advances in connectivity will enable seamless remote collaboration, building international partnerships and knowledge sharing.

19. How will regulations shape the digital economy?

Evolving policies on data privacy, digital currency, and AI ethics will protect users, encourage innovation, and ensure fair competition.

20. What is the vision for the digital economy's future?

The future digital economy will focus on sustainability, inclusivity, and ethical practices, creating opportunities and promoting prosperity for all.

Conclusion

The digital economy has reshaped our lives, work, and connections, creating a world that is more connected and innovative. This book explains the main elements of the digital economy, the key players involved, popular business models, and emerging technologies. It also covers important challenges, like privacy, cybersecurity, economic inequality, and environmental impact, and discusses trends for the future.

The digital economy brings new opportunities, allowing businesses to reach global audiences and offering people flexible work options. However, it also demands adaptability, continuous learning, and a focus on ethical behavior. As technology advances, it's essential to make sure the digital economy grows in a way that is inclusive, sustainable, and fair.

The digital economy is built on data and technology, covering areas like online shopping and finance, and adapts continuously to trends and consumer needs. New technologies, like AI and blockchain, require businesses, governments, and individuals to be ready for constant change and aware of the risks involved. The digital economy offers many opportunities, including flexible work options, remote jobs, and the ability for individuals and businesses to thrive globally.

To build trust and promote responsible growth, it is necessary to address risks like cybersecurity, data privacy, and fairness. The future vision for the digital economy emphasizes sustainability and inclusivity, with fair policies and equal access for all.

As we look to the future, the digital economy will continue to evolve, making it important for governments, businesses, and communities to work together to guide its growth in ways that benefit everyone and protect the environment.

www.ingramcontent.com/pod-product-compliance
Lightning Source LLC
Chambersburg PA
CBHW070940220526
45469CB00007B/2465